# A Handful of Bees

# A Handful of Bees

## poems by Dzvinia Orlowsky

*2/1/08*

*For Wardie,
With gratitude
for the many years
of knowing you,
& for the music
you brought to
our family,*

*Dzvinia*

**Carnegie Mellon University Press    Pittsburgh    2008**

## ACKNOWLEDGMENTS

These poems have appeared sometimes in different versions in the
following publications:

*AGNI:* "At the National Home," "In Winter," "Luba Doesn't
Have the Mouse," "The River," "A Handful of Bees," "The Joke;"
*Blur (Boston Literary Review):* "The Slaughter;" *Brix:* "The
Grotto at Lourdes;" *Embers:* "Barn Lumber," "Rifle;" *Green
Mountains Literary Review:* "View;" *Hayden's Ferry Review:* "At
the Cemetery;" *Jacaranda Review:* "Four in the Morning,"
"Yellow Jacket;" *Ploughshares:* "Anesthesia," "Praying;" *Plum
Creek Review:* "Her Back;" *Pocketpal:* "Sheep;" *Quarry West:*
"Daybreak;" *Sojourner:* "To Our Cosmeticians;" *Sycamore Review:*
"Our Grotto;" *The Beloit Poetry Journal:* "Burying Dolls;" *The
Journal:* "Morning," "Poland," "Recurrence;" *The Pennsylvania
Review:* "Occupation of the Deceased;" *Puerto Del Sol:* "First
Communion," "Poem For My Cat."

With deep gratitude to Jay Hoffman, Franz Wright, Askold
Melnyczuk, and Nancy Mitchell for their confidence; to Heather
McHugh and Gary Duehr for their intuitive help on the manuscrip
to Tamara Orlowsky, Catherine Sasanov, Gloria Mindock, Martha
McCollough, Jane Brox, and Russ Sully for their interest and
support; and to my sister, Maria, who with me every August still
looks for signs.

*A Handful of Bees* was originally published by Carnegie Mellon
University Press in 1994.

First Carnegie Mellon Classic Contemporaries Edition, May 2008

The publisher expresses gratitude to James Reiss,
James W. Hall, Jesse Lee Kercheval, and Louisa
Solano for their contributions to the Classic
Contemporaries Series.

Library of Congress Control Number 2007937624
ISBN 978-0-8748-485-8

10  9  8  7  6  5  4  3  2  1

# CONTENTS

## Prologue

III

In memory

of my father, Miroslaus Orlowsky

"Everything is an event for those who know how to tremble"

ॐ Jean Follain

# PROLOGUE

## Recurrence

### 1.

At first we allowed for coincidence:
The black telephone.
The rain.
The glass breaking on the floor.

We didn't want to believe you
even as we watched you pack.
Sometimes explanations fall short.

### 2.

Shadow on the X-ray.
I don't sleep,
only lie, pretending to sleep.

The lamp dimmed in another room,
Mother reading the medical journals
she hides under her pillow —

shadow across words
she doesn't understand.

### 3.

As for understanding,
it has to do with the concealed layout
of skin, the code within a drop of blood.
It's there, typed in a band of light
around your wrist.  Its script
is breath.

## Anesthesia

Count backwards: the moon
behind eyelids,

a small radio
pinned to your pillow.

They begin to descend,
one by one,

parachutists
carrying buckets of new blood.

One by one, the missing
check in.

## Our Grotto

Afraid of cries, or a growl from his throat,
I'd unlock the morphine
from its cool safe,
slide the needle
into the soft sag of muscle
curved below his hip.
I'd watch him grow quiet.

He'd grown so small
collapsed inside of himself,
I could have gathered him up in my arms
and carried him — a demolition of bones
I wanted to hide from priests
who'd pick through
the debris for sins.

The doctors sent him home to die.
Mother believed he'd live,
believed the nurse's optimism
with which my sister
brought him soda,
took his temperature.

Each morning as if to say
he still was with us,
Father's kidneys pumped
no matter what the women did
or didn't do.
How they nursed it, made it theirs —
this miracle they looked out for . . .

I

### Thunderbird

Mother takes the keys out of her bedroom dresser drawer,
asks me to start the Thunderbird.
I pump the gas petal, turn the ignition.

Each year the leather hat left on the dashboard
looks more dry, dust-infested.
We idle in the driveway.

Mother wants the top down.
The clasps jam and won't release.
She pounds with her palms against the canvas.

The convertible trunk automatically opens, lets in air.
The trunk slowly lowers again, four clicks
locking it into place.

## Visiting the Cemetery

She weeds the ground
for a vase of hyacinth
to be placed in front of his name.
She doesn't ask for my help.
Does she think only her hands (not mine)
can keep a promise?

## Morning

Nothing can disturb you now —
your sleep is the sleep
of a basin of water
where a woman
has washed her face.

This is the hour
of churchyard haze,
the pale pink sun
around heads of saints.
It must be their slow light
that carries here
to the grassfields, the cornfields,
the hand-carved wheat.

If only I could wake you!
The steam in barns has started to rise,
and there behind the wooden shed —
the last piece of moon
in an empty pail.

## Rifle

The dead buck hung
from a tree in our backyard —
a symbol of luck and good marksmanship.
Father stayed in bed, fevered head
burning like an anvil,
remembering how good it felt
to be hunting orange-vested
in the underbrush.
For weeks the hoofs
skimmed the snow,
and I'd hear the tree creak
under the weight.
As if to protect us,
Father racked the rifle above the fireplace,
leather-encased like a strong arm.

## Barn Lumber

Alone in New England, she could never love
the ocean as she loved fields —
barns collapsed into a wreckage
of windows and doors, without the man who sawed
and hammered their boards
into furniture,
whose shoulders Mother once
described as masculine.
I understand now, these reminders she keeps.
One, a barn lumber table
on which she burns a hurricane lamp.
Another, a rifle propped
against the window of her bedroom,
bulletless, but labeled with tape
marked "dangerous."

## Life Insurance

Father died of cancer — but
that's nobody's business.

I take a deep breath:
"There is no bad health history —
no mental illnesses, no back
trouble, no heart disease
or cancer, no.
His colon just stopped working."
The nurse looks up at me,
marks the application "1" for "liar."

"Any allergies?" she asks.
I turn milkweed white.
"Respiratory diseases?"
I look around the room.

And should I lie about the children I won't have?
Show her the doctor's scribble
of scarred tubes?
Father thought I was perfect.

"Any kids?"

She draws my blood over the kitchen table.
"It'll be a couple of weeks,"
she says without looking up,
confident in her one memorized fact.

## Occupation of the Deceased

My late father:  frog.
Or so Mother insists
on nights when she is lonely
and needs a sign
that he is still with us in this world
and cares enough to visit.

I tell her:  nonsense.
I cannot bear the thought of his eager
thumping forward in the grass.

5:00 AM, a light rainfall nourishes crickets.
Their ringing stops.
Whose company do I keep?

## Her Back

It seemed she was constantly near the ground,
pulling grass out, pushing seeds in.
She said I would warm my back in the sun.
I stood above her, in a sweatshirt,
wishing I was indoors.

Father taught me to run,
running kept his heart strong.
I impressed him running downhill.
My father loved strong limbs. I loved my father.

Company came, I wore long skirts.
We sat together and listened.
They came to eat dinner and to nap.
Someone's blond hair in my lap; I was afraid to move.
If I did, I knew I'd have to play the piano.

For years there was only one song.
Mother covered her laughter with one hand,
Father clapped. This year they were embarrassed.
Our dogs were kept locked in one room;
we smelled our hands after petting them.

The church burned down. It didn't seem right,
although I was never fond of going. There,
hands in white gloves, lips quivering,
the old women all looked alike — all my grandma,
kneeling from beginning to end.

## In Winter

Grandpa's penis hung,
a withered mushroom
from balls still sprouting
a few white hairs.
His ass was a courier's
weathered leather bag —
empty of mail.

Not that I have proof.
But it had to be true —
the way Grandma spit
whenever he came near.

Yet, in winter,
when the stove went out,
she'd undress, her nipples
dark, sad as prunes,
and she'd turn toward him
remembering how coal was once
worth freezing her hands to find.

II

## First Communion

These never fall: the crucifix
pinned like a tailless kite
above church doors, Virgin Mary's
out-turned hands, raised and weightless,
Christ down on one knee in stained glass...

The sacrament blazes and dies,
and the heart left starved for more suffering
becomes god-like — This

drew me further across the parking lot
of gravel and grass to a playground
where belly-flopped across a swinging seat
I became an angel, suspended
over mud, a tornado twisting
the steel chains into a helix
until I'd lift both feet and lose control.

## Praying

The priest taught us
that blessing oneself
shouldn't be like shooing flies:

there is a pause
at the temple of your head;

you connect one shoulder
to the other with a thread;

your wrist should be sincere
as if conducting your body
in song.

. . .

On long car trips
it's okay

to pray while driving,
your lips parted,

hands resting
on the steering wheel.

Soon, however,
you're falling asleep.

The rosary breaks
and spills into trees.

Feeling guilty
for asking too many favors

I disguise myself
by praying with my mother's accent.

Maybe for her
salvation will be gentle —

dawn pausing to empty
birds from a gray sack.

## The Grotto at Lourdes

I dip my fingers into the font,
lightly touching the water

as if the face
of God slept there

and couldn't be disturbed.
The earth too

waits to be touched.
We're grateful to dip

into the river,
the reflection of trees.

Inside the cathedral,
prayers released,

we expose ourselves
deformed, insane,

then sign the cross three times,
as if sewing ourselves up,

as if only one stitch
wouldn't be strong enough.

## Poem for My Cat

Your time was up
when you crossed the road —

though I wasn't sure,
afraid to look.

Here keecha.
Come keecha.

"Ivan" my father named you
though it would have been more fun

to name you Volodimir,
after the Horrible,

who (struck down, beheaded)
could still get up and run.

There were many black male cats
in Brunswick, unexplained sounds,

eight more lives to go around.  Surely
you would come back...

But after that, everything that moved
wasn't you.

## At the National Home

By 36, I'd outlived Mozart.
My life had accumulated its own Weltschmertz:
divorce, an early prognosis of blindness,
(hysteria, Mother said, runs in the family)
all brought to the piano, prominent and open
like a coffin.

We were promised one genius per family.
In dreams, my hand turns the page
to the one song I know:  Venetian Boat Song.
Raising and pressing the foot pedal,
the water laps, the gondolier dips his oar.

But fingers know their limitations.
At the Ukrainian National Home,
ankle-socked and with a tight braid
coiled to my head, I lost the rhapsody
Liszt might have felt; I sat numb
before the backdrop of Carpathian Woods.

By the time I finished playing,
Father had excused himself,
his empty seat raised.
A large fan blew the scent
of children waiting next in line
to shame their parents, then take a bow.

## Sheep

Sheep ruin the grass for horses.
Their determination is
to move like clouds
one by one
in loose groups.

In cold rain they are a crowd
waiting for an angel to appear
on a leafless bush.

In bright daylight
you'll see them glistening
on hillsides; at night
they try to absorb the moon.

Sleepwalkers, they never
stop counting themselves to themselves.

## First Generation

It was good to be first at something

even if it meant parents
who by speaking

shut out the world
except for my sister, and me

and Bimko, our dog,
who understood bilingual commands.

    . . .

They looked like white birds
assembling in our shopping center parking lot

We imagined their crosses burning
smoke twisting through lawns across town

almost beautiful

    . . .

Swapping pure for pure
we changed our names

In school I became "Peggy"
My dolls listened and never blinked

Our neighbor, a farmer, combed our ten acres
to look more like Ohio

In exchange, we gave him our dog

Back to Us

Hard to believe one horse could cause
so much trouble — standing motionless in the yard,
a bucket of water next to it,

tail lifted and arched, eyes fixed ahead,
what it couldn't use
about to be given back to us.

No one could work near the hay bales.
Hurdles of dust, they'd make us itch
just to look at them.  Father complained

about the pollen that blew into the living room.
When we forgot to close the door behind us,
flies followed us in, driving Mother crazy

until she offered us a penny for each fly killed.
With swift cruelty, we squashed them
with the edge of a curtain

or suffocated them with a glass
pressed against the window pane.
That's how they'd die —

stiff, and in good enough shape:
we could pick one up by the corner of a wing,
look at it, swear it had a face, and feel bad.

## The River

ॐ after Alexander Dovzhenko (1894-1956), Ukrainian filmmaker

Half a century later
it was still spring.

The hanged turned their heads up
to look at the swaying sky,

and the one-eyed man
continued to be king.

Then night came:

horses kicked up dust
from beneath their stables,

and the moon tossed children
back to their sleeping mothers.

It was not a flood
that destroyed the village,

but fire, the forest —

Only a river continued to flow
through Dovzhenko's journals,

a clear glass vein.

### Burying Dolls

The camps have long stopped burning
when Mother toasts my birth with cognac;
Father films, the dog sniffs my crib.

Barbie is sent to work camp in my closet.
The officers like her pony tail.
Ask Mother.
Ask her how they'll come at night
to choose their women.

My children will bury
dolls in the garden,
whisper masses for processions of shoe boxes.
I'll tell them:  women have to look strong
to stay alive.

Ask Grandmother.
Watch her every morning
lightly slap her face
to give it color.

## Poland

The light on Mother's face
divides her in half.
Outside a garden hides its shadow,
a summer blouse
folded once. The moon guides light,
thread sliding through
the silver eye
or the thin white blood
of the Eucharist:
some eternal secret
passes from hand to mouth.
I want to feel the interiors
of churches,
breath of stone,
ancestors I can't touch.
So I watch the sleep
of my mother's face.

## Luba Doesn't Have the Mouse

How dumb of the teacher
to assume that we, third graders,
imprisoned in so small a classroom
every Saturday while other children played,
forced by our parents to love
the old country we cared little for,
had a mouse.

It was Luba's turn to recite a poem.
We memorized one a week,
our tongues rolling
on unfamiliar ground.

Seeing her with two braids and thick glasses,
a big goof reciting a poem about how
the children of the Ukraine never forget,
was too much to ask for,
too much to take.

We began to make squeak sounds,
to break the trance
that brought her nearer
to the poem's end.
"Luba maye mishkoo," we droned.
Luba has a mouse.

We must've assumed
the teacher was deaf —
every day she stood numb
before the blackboard,
bewildered,
the world

kneaded into one
incomprehensible pile of dough
it was her responsibility
to unfold and cut into meaningful
shapes for us.

"Give me the mouse!"
She turned a boiled ham pink.
Not even Luba's tears spared us our punishment:
one hundred times
in seven tenses, "Luba has a mouse."

That morning
it took us longer
than usual to settle down —
to open our books to a map of a country
resembling a puddle
labelled "bread basket of the world."

Impossible to say whether or not
the teacher ever forgave us
for stealing the clapper
out of the bell.

Or if we learned anything —
if repeating
the past, present,
and future
one hundred times
ever answered the question...

## Cousins

The first writes to say
he can repair anything

The second cousin phones:  he's just arrived

The third is one of many
in the photograph's black and white orchard of faces

A fourth asks:  do we need gold?
His is a mouthful of metal

The fifth cousin sends me a small peasant woman made of wood
She is a box that when opened reveals a smaller woman
who when opened reveals a smaller woman...

A sixth cousin waves goodbye like an astronaut
a VCR tied to his back

The seventh cannot go

He begs:  please for my wife
and points to a wig

All this can't be family

## The Joke

America split her gut
when he came looking for work.

So he dissects himself into small piles: factory worker,
philosopher, lover of books. He cuts further: eyes,
mouth. . . visa . . .

Only what's essential
placed on a scale.

But because he's family, we insist on gifts:
ties flocked with succulent geese,
big cadillac shoes,

the joke shop soap that never lathers.

Never mind the beef like a cow's
forehead hammered soft, resting
on the refrigerator shelf,

a dish of blood pooled beneath it.
He won't touch it
though you thought: *he wants* red meat.

Guilt seated him
at the head of our table,
placed the knife's long stomach
next to his plate . . .

But abstinence remained his gracious host.

It gave him less to pack,
and more of himself to take home.

## When First Stars Appear

My sister ties her apron, tests
the boiled cabbage with her fork,
waits for each large leaf to pull away.

Mother sits at the dinner table
guarding the candle lit for the dead.
This is not her country.
Every Epiphany she reminds us
how she lost everything.

The Bandurist Choir struggles to be heard —
the stereo needle dragging its wad of dust . . .
This year, who will praise their voices,
their dead gifts?

She tells us the same fable
of how at midnight barn animals speak . . .
My embroidered shirt irritates my neck.

Did you feed them?
Give them water?
Did you cause them pain?

I listen each time knowing
it is never the animals
that complain.

III

## A Handful of Bees

By chance, in mirrors, I've noticed that when I eat,
it's often with a facial expression
of disbelief.

Isn't the food mine?
Why do I hurry?
Will I be divorced again?

When my mother eats,
it's often with a facial expression
of disbelief.

Isn't the food hers?
Why does she hurry?
Is Father dying again?

Why does she tighten her left hand
into a fist?
It gets tighter all the time.

Will the fist become mine?
What does it know?
What's there that can't be released?

## You Threaten to Have a Stroke but Instead I Do

First you cry and clench your fist.
Then I cry and blow my nose.

Who said once in a while
it's good to have these arguments?
I pass you your purse.
You pass me a glass of water.

We want to think it can be endured:
the heart exposed . . .

But what of the brain?
Its vessels like couriers
working over-time.

And what of logic, its runt?
Better to be done with it.
The day ended with an exclamation point,

leaving me speechless with one functioning arm
and two faces:  one alert and forgiving,
the other, like yours.

## Self-Portrait

Behind door number one
nothing

Behind door number two
nothing

Behind door number three
a large mirror

## To Our Cosmeticians

1.

You want us to believe
there are only two kinds of women:
the Before
and the After.

In the Before Woman's life
it's always raining.
If you blow on her,
a parachute desperately opens.

She has no lips to speak of.


2.

Turn the page
and the After Woman appears.

She survives the hijacking of her heart.
She is match-lit.

Her blush is the red of a bull's death.
Her hair bounces back for more.

She's been known to bite.

3.

If you ask me what season I am,
I would say late fall —
just at that time
when trees give up
and drop their leaves.

My best colors are:

file cabinet,
highway,
Ohio,

I wear them the way
the wind wears what it passes.

I like my meek mouth,
my no-grapes-on-the-stem look.
It makes me hirable.


4.

But thank you
for your day of beauty.

If I change my skin
it'll be gradual,

the rest of my life.

## View

Mornings are exhausting — we get
dressed in our work clothes;
there is no inspiration,
no matter how directly the sun shines
on sidewalks, no matter how many nursemaids
stroll with navy-blue perambulators
under bare park trees — despite, that is,
all those serious babies.

The trick is not to be sidetracked,
not to be fooled by monuments
dedicating spring to soldiers,
or by gardens potted on
long private terraces.

By the end of the day
only buses know their destinations,
only ambulances believe
the urgency of their abrupt horns,
while we return to separate rooms,
the same view outside of window,
favorite paragraph, favorite book,
night after night . . .

Is there something there
worth remembering —
white quilt of snow in the courtyard,
benches, shadows of benches,
trees, shadows of trees?

## Yellow Jacket

You were probably no more
than a moment's bad temper on wings,
a piece of an afternoon's shrapnel.

But I cursed you
for disturbing my reading,
slowing your jets
around my ankles and feet.

Until now, I could have said
I'd never killed anything.
Anything, at least,
that took less than a second to die.

I didn't mean for you to end up
a motionless knot
on the floor.

I could've *used* a sting,
the reassurance
that in other worlds
purpose still exists,

even if only to have
set fire to my skin;
I could've carried that throb
like neon

to my heart,
a gift of lightning
for what cannot fly.

## A Minute Ago

everything was fine.
Now the trees bend a little more,

a little more black.  Even the chair
(to be thrown out) curves into a grin.

My sister, a nurse, asks over the phone:  does it pucker
or does it float?

I touch it slowly.
My husband is asleep, a newspaper covering his face.

Would he remarry?  Have children late in life?
What do I fear?  Am I an other

woman who'll want more and more,
who already exists —

but one his fingers don't yet know?

## On Our Street

You just don't get it
is what the school teacher meant
when she told me I might enjoy
repeating the class

is what the piano teacher thought
when he closed the music book
and asked if I'd ever
considered dancing

is what the ballet teacher instinctively knew
when she put me in the last row —
where I tried to hold my pose, leg dangling
like a broken umbrella

is what the GRE score card told me
because I compared apples to oranges,
said stones are to branches
as leaves are to sky —

one can not touch the other —
is what I meant to say to my first husband
when he told me to leave, and I packed and left for good
having said nothing, and a neighbor

waved as I pulled up to the sign
**DEAF CHILD SLOW BLIND CHILD**

## Switchboard

Just when I thought
I was going to be put on hold,
I got cut off.

Just when I was beginning to believe
all messages are saved (pink paper:
called to see you,
wants to see you)
I got quiet.

Now there is no one,
except the number dialed,
the voice that reassures me
at the tone there is time.

Telephones:  technology
incapable of simple conversation.

Savored strangers,
cut off and dimeless, each one
an astronaut lost.

It's not my fault
I was assigned this job
so soon after my divorce.

Who engineered these intricate bridges?
They collapse under my supervision.
My head won't connect with my heart.

## Four in the Morning

"If white ants feel fine at four in the morning,
let's congratulate the ants."

                            Wislawa Szymborska

But first, let's congratulate my nerves
for chewing through
the last leaf of sleep.

Moth, deft as a thumb,
hanging on my white gauze curtain,
let me join you.
Together, let's pound
our powdered wings;
grow fat

on the prospect of light.
At four in the morning,
white ants do fine
hoeing the cool sands
of their kingdom.
They love their chores

begun before day itself begins —
disembalming cherries,
confiscating rain,
traversing the earth
weightless, carrying their dead,
lighter still.

## The Slaughter

My eyes recognize
their own animal.  Its gaze is
brown-stained, ready.

The alarm shoots its bullet —
but I've been awake
counting hours slept,
watching dawn dispel
what night wouldn't keep.

Maybe tomorrow I can start over
turned toward spring —
away from the mirror,
the dung, the hay.

## Daybreak

Dreamers cruise down country roads,
headlights spinning a thousand threaded lights.
Earth pauses for those waking, for the sleepless

to shut off their alarms, for the insane to close
their long illegible letters.
I hear this house breathe,

it is my breath.  I listen —
there are loud sounds
and there are no sounds.

They meet at the bottom of the stairs.